Her Yes

Her Yes

POEMS BY
KIM VAETH

Zoland Books
CAMBRIDGE, MA

First Edition published in 1994 by
Zoland Books, Inc.
384 Huron Avenue
Cambridge, MA 02138

FIRST EDITION

This book has been printed on acid-free paper, and its binding materials have been
chosen for strength and durability.

ACKNOWLEDGMENTS

Grateful acknowledgment is made to the editors of the following magazines,
in which these poems first appeared, sometimes in earlier versions: *Open
Places,The Women's Review of Books, Ploughshares,The American Voice,The
Queen's Quarterly,13th Moon,The Kenyon Review*

My deepest thanks go to Mildred Bissinger, Kathleen Fraser, Jean Valentine,
and Marilyn Hacker.

And to the Virginia Center for the Creative Arts, the MacDowell Colony and
Yaddo for their generous support during the writing of many of these poems.

LIBRARY OF CONGRESS CATALOGING-IN-PUBLICATION DATA

Vaeth, Kim. 1952-
    Her yes : poems / by Kim Vaeth. — 1st ed.
      p. cm.
    ISBN 0-944072-40-2
    I. Title
    PS3572. A34H47   1994
811' .54 — dc20   93-40518
                                         CIP

Book designed by Jeanne Abboud

PRINTED IN THE UNITED STATES OF AMERICA

for their yes, I dedicate this book to
my mother, Barbara Joynes Twine
and my aunt, Florence Joynes Stewart

Contents

Part One

Wild Strawberries   3

Part Two

Why Didn't They Hear The Sea Calling?   11
Willoughby, Virginia   12
Elsinore   15
The Beauty of It   16
Entering the Clear Space   17
The Dream   18
A Flute in the Middle of the Night   19
Akhmatova's Voice   21
Wanting What Is Barely Seen   22

Part Three

Here   25
Pencil and Blue Crayon   26
Speeding North In June   27
Here Is My Kiss   28

Friendship Among Women   29
The Bath   36
Waiting For Jazz   38
Pear As Pear   39
The Yes   40

Part Four

Mrs. Einstein   43
The Voice of the Painter   46
What the Wings Look Like   47
Transportation   48
One Hour of Joy   49
At the End of the Cold War   50
Steiglitz Marries Her Hands   51
Tonight I Am Mrs. Lorca   52
Which Wants To   53

Part Five

Falling Into and Out of   57
Grief   60
Inland Beachchair   63
Shapes   64
The New City   65
Look   66
Water of Praise   67
A Flock of Doubts Flying Beyond the Given Boundaries   70

Notes   72

Part One

Wild Strawberries

I am here as a dreamer, where the old city
meets a geometric wilderness, the awkward figure
in the landscape, painted

almost by chance by the painter
who hopes
I lean over a balcony, my own life perhaps, and the blue

hope beyond, enter the sea naked
I swim out into all the green
cool water parts between viaducts whose trains

flash through the sun it's possible to think
in pictures and live many lives.
Summer passes, armies thrive and uranium

travels east in boxcars, our lives
are red
umbrellas

open against the glare of a nordic heatwave. We
lean over our private balconies
into the same future.

ᔓ

Begin by asking
ridiculous things
of the past.

A long sleep and then
waking with an intense
hunger for an uneaten meal.

lust like black and white

Allow me to love
all of you —
it could go on for years.

This loyalty
is like blindness.

lust for vision and sight

There are men who go blind
in combat. Preparing myself
for that moment when everything goes

not black
but back.

Dancing along and suddenly
snow in the mountains!
A familiar and physical place becomes

unknown shapes. May I always see
the little mirrors sewn
into cloth.

Not subject but color —
Costakis said later
in Greece.

Pastured out to another
language, pictures
on the reverse side of the eye.

mystic light of the bright summer night

I like a horizon, the granite side
of the slope, nude women
and coffee from china

cups.

∽

Flowers arrived from Australia
where it's winter, one works hard
in a short season. Another darling

on a train to Italy, promised love
and clinging at the station.
I think of you, walking around

in your light body, sweet belly
shining through the cars, people, ultramarine
sea, especially the sea, drinking

something red, something
white sleeping
astonishing aliveness!

Casa Bella Donna is dirty
but cheap, you write, *a special bird singing*
without pauses. A very little

wind makes our white
curtain move, the island she
is a beauty. I like the Italians

but Greece is in my
heart. Your light beautiful
body, Etruscan

Hellenic.
Peregrines on their way
to Africa, a paradise.

A mouthful of parsley and waving with Ella
Fitzgerald in a parade, dreams
and gardens provide

an older woman in purple
skirt and blouse, a green hat
an artist at the lighthouse!

∽

Emptiness bordering on something
else, why don't you write
something funny!

Things shift perceptibly
and imperceptibly, as in the soul
crossing that continental

divide where the rivers
flow in the other direction.
What you don't pass

through your soul
doesn't exist.
Half lives, my mother

slashing the tires of my airplane
while another girl, a German tourist, is named
after a song and well loved.

We only wanted to get away, only escape and arrive
safely, nothing else, wrote Anne Frank from her
Amsterdam attic.

Peregrines
seduced by air
cold sea, limbo

or whales. Shift the burden
of proof
upon those who want to kill

your light Etruscan beautiful
body.
Are we darlings together?

A word like *incisive*
speeds through the mind, unconscious
of origins, oh

I love you, my slalom course
at night without skis through packs of wild
animals. You

just left
on a train with your lover, new,
who instinctively grasps all my

failures. Huddled through
winter, a dream of past
strawberries and future

love. Living
dangerously an illusion
of speed, of courage.

The charm of the guitar
disappears. Little by little
listen, move

at my own pace.
Wearing clothes
of someone I don't love

smells bad, empty
give them
up and stay

cold. Wars rage
over wars. A Soviet
violinist

defects from the decadent
east to the decadent
west.

It's not that a place
belongs to us
but that we

resist the right things!
Live not what you saw.
You see.

Part Two

Part Two

Why Didn't They Hear The Sea Calling?

I was there riding in my mother's
car with father who was
driving. We got lost
and my mother asks — Honey, why don't we
pull into a gas station and ask?   My father refuses.
He says he'll find the right
street in just a minute.
He says he knows
right where it is.
Why didn't he hear
the sea calling to us, always
so close it was always living
so close.
Why weren't they drawn to it
like lovers swimming out and out?

Willoughby, Virginia

My grandmother
writes plays
in my dreams, with a cancer

I am afraid of
since now it's the truth.
She writes

alone at night
in her kitchen by the Chesapeake.
Her lamplight

is yellow, as if
painted by Vuillard.
The rest of the house

is dark. I use the spare key kept always
in the small wooden box beside the back door.
She hands me

the play.
As we embrace
I can feel my small breasts

push into the hollows
right through the air
where her large breasts used to be.

The only way I know
it is death
is that there is

no next time.
Come back, come back
my love will bring you back.

~

Sun on our
shoulders, snow
in our boots

further and further
into the bright world
the beauteous fields.

It was April. Easter.
I was in your
country.

I met Rosie
whom you loved and Maria who loved
you. We drove out of the city to go swimming.

The three of you giggled in Greek
and you threw a sea urchin at me.
I tried

to catch it and screamed
with pain. We drew
closer after that.

~

Always going forward
Bring me home.
A place for the quiet child

waiting in the corner
of her body, a reminder

the writing of every poem, drawing
says this is all I can be.
Night after night,

I return home, without
dreaming, to the two of them,
together, turning

on the lamp in the kitchen.
What will we do
in the name of love?

Elsinore

I keep my good eye on the watchtower and in the weeds.
In the heart. That wide, once sunny courtyard
now overgrown with murders. Lust that failed to turn generous.
Long, unheated halls. Evaporated attentions. Thick windows

facing the rocks. Beyond the rocks, the sea and Sweden.
It's cold love being a tourist. With my mother and beloved
who won't merge. I want to belong to them but they look
past me for relief. All this hiding myself

behind the drapes. I dream about my father's whispers.
Not the castle. Though dreaming of so many rooms by the sea
would free me to roam the inside kingdom.
But I take incest and murder literally. Not dreamtime.

The rage is not belonging anywhere. The rage is inheriting
the outside kingdom. All those rooms and hallways.

The Beauty of It

My father is sixty-six years old and I have always wanted him
to put his arms around me and hold me
for a long couple of minutes.
This hug could happen anywhere for no reason
and that's the beauty of it—
in his living room with all the windows,
in the parking lot at Be-Low's Grocery,
or on the beach at 52nd Street where we've walked
so many times. We'd stand there
without any shame. Without any fear
about what someone watching might think.
Without any regrets for it not happening sooner.
He would hold me and let himself
be held. I would do the same.
And there would be no rushing to get through it.
Nothing that was more important than this hug
which would say things no one ever told either of us
we could say to each other and survive.

Entering the Clear Space

You are that uncomplicated

    "jar of air"
    "door partly open"
    leaf lit from inside
    book of embraces

In this second and growing life —
you are that one child, that only forgiveness

who is with you as yourself and cannot hide.

The Dream

for Madeleine M. Kunin

When Susan photographed my hands
I wept. For myself. My childhood
ripped away. Anger lodged
in my throat. Afraid to see
how much silence is like speech — the dream
of being loved and accepting it. For my friends,
little stars in the Big Dipper —
swallowing more pain than light.
For the President who looks like a boy
the world never stripped of anything.

And she said from the shards:
we are precious there is courage there is justice

A Flute in the Middle of the Night

In December, I wrote *I am drowning*
in ice. Now it is
April. I am still writing.

      ∾

I put the irises in water and leave them
in the kitchen overnight. In the morning
I place them just outside the front door,
for it is cool there.
They are guests.

      ∾

the possibility of jumping
no one saw her

the possibility of midair
suspension of belief

the possibility of water
no one saved her

bridge of rain, give her
what she thinks she wants

      ∾

What happens in mid-

winter was nothing
but a trampoline

air?
In midair is it still

is it still pounding in you what
is pounding in you now
besides your heart?

～

It is after work, I am
drinking tea where

are you they found

your car. My lungs
ache *I see*
it is because *your eyes* I am alive
that I am confused.

～

In the morning, you told me
that while I slept, you played

your flute. I never heard you
play your flute — I never

heard you.

～

It is so simple, she said. Flowers
are not for us or the bees,
they are for themselves.

Akhmatova's Voice

Outside this alcove, the storm expected later arrives now,
a lush wet nearness in the pines after inconsolable heat that brushed
a life clear to its bone, the one I hold in my palm
unlike anything I know how to hold.
From the upper attic of my chest this life becomes song and the echoes
of songs belonging to other lives. The voice in the storm,
    Akhmatova's voice,
threads distance and time like the eight strokes of the Chinese
    character *forever,*
when she asks *who can refuse to live her own life?*

Whatever did not open
when I desired it so fiercely. Whatever was withdrawn
because it could not be imagined. Whatever was left unsaid out of fear
that gripped from the beginning. Whatever touch was held back
out of cowardice or absence of hope. Whatever was misunderstood
not out of failure but an unwillingness to know.
Whatever I have turned away from in the moment
I was most needed. Whoever has turned away from me,
I turn now toward each one.
Can you hear the turning?
The rustle of language just before language.

Wanting What Is Barely Seen

It's time to leave the road of injury
which brought us each part of the way

and still we are magnificent.

The poet, says "Yield everything. Force nothing."

Who will buoy me up?

Here I am in my own skin, trans-
luscent marrow
not waiting, not hiding

pure beauty.

Part Three

Here

Eye to eye, three wild roses
bloom in a glass of water
on my table, as supple
and near as you were
three hours ago. The rose in the middle
opens so fully it pulls
the entire stem and the two
buds over in an arch
with its faint pink weight,
calling perhaps to the meadow
it was once a part of —
summer here now.
Just as your recent
cries still reverberate
along my throat, this wild
rose creates a stirring
in me, a raw hope,
a hummingbird, unexpected
yet here, sacred. Rising
from nothing I know
about the past, rising
from a ripe blood orange.

Pencil and Blue Crayon

Let the last drawing I make with pencil and blue crayon
be of you in the bath.

Let the weather be fine in February and August.

Let all of us belong to the sunlit now and move
from surprise to surprise.

Let the yellow dining rooms where we drink wine
have red tablecloths and balconies.

Let all I cannot say open me in your arms.

Let me sit in an old beachchair touching the green present.

Speeding North In June

On and off all day I've imagined your birthday
and the party your friends are probably giving you.

I'm there, off-center, drinking
the hairtonic your country sips to extreme,

a woman under your influence
prolonging her pain.

My mind types brief messages
which, fifty years ago, would have been telegramed

with **STOP** at the end of each pared down remark.
Instead, I'll reel you in like a fish with music

that matters. It's beautiful here. I'm not exactly lonely
but your dry laugh and unpredictable hair slip into me at times.

Nothing's the same and that's the poetic process. You know nothing
about the redhead I try to make a new start with

or how I wake up early to dig out my red car from the snow.
The rose sofa with ivory flowers is new and my sister

is in love with a man who's been married three times.
Haven't we all in the latter half of the century?

I've been more desperate, more obscure than I am now watching you
lift upward, evaporate lightly, as if you were nothing

but air, water, molecules
as if you were gone, as if I were enough without you.

Here Is My Kiss

Here is everything
I have made in my life so far.

Lip and
blossom and blossom
erupt. Little tornado of touch
as bluejay touches birch
in sexual honeysuckle now.
Thick paint and love inside us, my love!

Friendship Among Women

— we enter and it is our home
MARY OPPEN

1

In a strange city, remote, British, yet barely hanging on,
we are here at the edge.

What is asked while closing the door, while turning the corner?

Your child is asleep with her last question. By day, I can only
manage poor explanations of things I have never understood. Still,
she holds my hand, asks for lullabyes.

You let her interrupt us. "It is easier," you say like a bribe.

I am not used to interruptions. I have long silences whenever I want.
No child. "I live my life like a meditation," I say to you.
We are not envious of each other. We learn about our pasts
by listening to the other's explanations to the child, the child.

I am here in this city. You live three thousand miles east in another.
It is only in the woods that you remark, "things are much damper
here."

My project for this trip is to draw everything I kiss. Emily Dickinson,
hardbound, props the window open.

Now think of the islands, the new and empty landscapes I could have
on any one of them. The weather that could easily change.

2

In the morning, I try to hold onto certain things, the way I want
to hold you and not hold back anymore.

The white sheet strewn over the naked body. Falling in and out
of sleep, the room becomes lighter and lighter and lighter. Try
to imagine the curve of a shoulder you could love. This part is
a film. Sit through me twice.

Sleep gives me back to myself. In the deep privacy of sleep, we are
taken away from each other as if over a bridge, down a ladder.
The act of sleep unnerves me, carries me into the middle of my own
life.

A dark drive home, peculiar seeping coldness at three
in the morning. Pulling away from the curb. You stand in your
doorway, facing the street. For the first time all night, you are in my
peripheral vision. Because I want you so much, you slip away.

Quickly, the breath drawn in. Form a word. A word that will let you
know I don't believe in loneliness. Quickly: my face.

All summer you disappear and emerge from the fog.
By September, my hands are wings. It was one of those warm
afternoons in paradise when you walked over and began to talk
about generosity.

3

Rain. Tonight you talked about killing people in order
to feed people. During the meal, our private thoughts
on starvation, the various forms of hunger.

We walk all over the neighborhood twice, until two in the morning.
You pause with each cigarette to light a match
in the rain, my wool coat smelling more and more like an animal.

"You are desperate," is the first things you tell me, though you are
the one who will later move from far below the equator
into the snow. Recognition amongst refugees.

Your mother is a philosopher. On Christmas Day you ask me over
and over, until I consent, to cut your long black hair.
"Like a man's," you say. You swim in the ocean to celebrate.

Around you I laugh and retreat, laugh and rest, laugh and cry.
Around you, the feeling persists that I was, once,
wiser than I am now. Late at night, you play the guitar and sing
your own language.

In translation, the name of the man you love means: *flower*.
A political prisoner since the age of 18, he eventually "forgot
how to laugh," you explain.

You are a married woman with a new country. Here are
the photographs of the two of you in the snow. The town
is in the distance, like your husband. You are still yourself.
I am still.

4

Things persist. Twice a week, in February, we sat in the same
room. At first, this room seemed ugly. Other things also changed.
For instance, each day grew longer.

We listened to each other, the writing, the room, it was bright and we
each thought, *smart*, without concentrating. Then we saw our red
and black handwriting and later, the green apple going into your mouth
and in April, we noticed a little sunburn on my cheeks but didn't think
of kissing then.

We thought of it while drawing a picture with charcoal.
"A glass of wine?" We said yes, yes, yes and were girls together
that night in May.

It released easily between and within us, within and between. We
were falling out of our chairs. Our socks were flying. We were laughing
the great laugh of the ones who want to climb in the sunny hills.

The soft hills of blue powder that we are pulled into, in love, our
mother on the french fence, soft hair, maybe thinking the same thing
only earlier.

Everything there is to think about. Diving into the cold waves. For
example: who we love. Further. Driving through the fields, fruit,
summer. Knowing something about how the best in our life transpires
while watching small birds fly low over the river.

Where now is the city? It is gone from us. Nothing but the density
of friends sitting around in rooms thinking about brightness, the lamps
off. Almost dark now at eight o'clock. Two orange towels
on the clotheslines. A few children. The same dog jumping over
the same fence.

5

Early August. Besides each other, we have met no women traveling
alone.

Sitting together in the whitewashed room at four in the morning, your
cigarette burning above the end of the bed. Just outside the door,
music and the laughter of men to whom almost everything belongs.

Where are we now? The present moment: this island.

Lying there in the dark field beside the water. What are you thinking
when the forlorn bicycle rolls by under the cypress trees, its light
a slow quiet push. Do you feel it too? The past pouring in.

What did I eat? What dream and smell are mine? What bed,
what place did I know? Everywhere is the sea.

Then suddenly: the largest falling star we have ever seen is there
above us. Is gone. "Does the whole star fall?"

"When is the next boat?" "Where will I sleep tonight?"
"Are you hungry?" I agree to wire money I borrowed
to your grandmother's bank in Paris.

Kiss. Kiss. Each soft cheek. We separate. Goodbye. Goodbye.
Turn, sink into the crowd. The void enfolds and that delicate nausea,
fingering my ticket.

We disappear into boats going in opposite directions.
By the mouth of the harbor, once again, women traveling alone.

6

The swift move to kiss the face and lie down. Not the joy of talking
but to see your eyes light up close. Without many friends,
I'm determined and afraid at that looming hour when I return to bed.
"Bad dream. Fire." In a few hours, you're combing your wet hair
in the light beside me. "Aren't I close?" you ask, expecting yes.

I watch you empty. Birds. Waves. Thin lines of molecules
in the sky. Smaller gestures. Cold black rocks
carried hand to hand. Loss of hunger for food. Watching your face
in the bath, I feel my slender freedom. Another soul
stolen by the wind.

The unconscious leans in, fluorescence through the window
of the shortest day. Slices of raw ginger destined for the soup.
Little driftwood fires beside the ocean.

Music and being all the way alive. Thinking about the next time
without ever really knowing. Row to shore now and don't be sorry.
Turn on the lamps. Feel deeply. Lie down. Or get up early and go off
together.

7

Light with a deep reverence for life and dreams not to be betrayed.
Becoming. Water poured into one jar. Not so precise, yet
uninterrupted clarity, promise. An awkwardness triumphs into
something else. Absence or longing transformed. That late
willingness to fail and then courage. So soothing until
the next time. The body of yesterday's rose
still carried through the streets circuitously toward home
and open hands. The water and the jar. During the day,
during the night.

The Bath

Only the sound of you

        splashing while I shift

                from foot to foot in the cold

kitchen where the windows

        have frosted so I can't see out.

                I pull the string overhead and light

floods the cold, hard surfaces

        each time, too bright.

                You are taking one of your famous

baths, as you do

        when you are tired or cold

                or uneasy in the night. Newly washed,

your red hair, your red hair

        sings to me

                through the closed door and the steam

which seeps out

        under it.

I know it is late but your hair

is not tired.   And though I am very

cold, I am happy

being sung to.

Soon, but not yet,

I will walk into the bathroom,

sit down on the blue toilet seat

and ask you something.

You in the tub,

naked and wet, your skin

shining and freckled,

your eyes closed, your glasses far away

in another room, your singing hair

swept back by water,

converging where your nape

curves into the tub's curve, a thin washcloth

spread over your chest.

Waiting For Jazz

You were waiting for jazz. I was waiting for you.
Snow on the newest green leaves during your two hour
absence. I bathe. Unlonely with a music I can touch.
I walk privately through the city in your grandfather's
clothes. Turning my face to the sun, as though the winter
had been very long, very serious. Singing: *love and be loved.*

Pear As Pear

Little pear tree
teach me tonight
sweet columbine-in-the-dark

Now
I see the cup as cup
and you as you

my new

branch, simple in our blue kimonos
the night
wears on, moving
in, under
sleepless, sleepless hours
little pear tree
teach me tonight
sweet columbine-in-the-dark
Yes
I see the pear as pear
and you as you

The Yes

Because you have opened

and opened me, I am trying to enter an old fear.
I leave the circle
of the bed and walk out into the middle of the field
where you said yes. For a long time
I look at the stars. Then feel for
the buckles along the leather straps. Unfasten
them, pull them over my head. The bit falls
from my mouth. Feel their old weight
in my hands, lay them down in the brown
suddenly delicious grass. Turn around under the stars
and walk back slowly
toward the dark stable.

Part Four

Mrs. Einstein

The Genius

Many said that he was a possessed genius
and that such genius left no room for the trivia of life.
His genius is recognized by its fallibilities —
the socks he forgot to wear to dinner parties,
the sixth grade arithmetic problems he got wrong.
Albert Einstein rode a bicycle to relax.
We try to make this genius palatable.
We want him to be one of us.
We study his brain.

Those who knew him observed:

As his mind knows no limits, so his body follows no set rules.
He sleeps until he is awakened.
He stays awake until he is told to go to bed.
He will go hungry until he is given something to eat
and then he eats until he is stopped.

This is about Mrs. Einstein
how she told him these things, day after day
how Mrs. Einstein made room.

The Special Theory of Relativity

Mrs. Einstein asks her friends what this theory means
because she is so fond of the word *relativity*.

Hannah mentions thermodynamics
Greta mentions energy
Clara says, *it is everything*
not only in this world, Elsa, but in this universe.

TIME AND SPACE

Elsa wonders if the grass is relative to the sky the sky
to the Alps the Alps to the stars the stars
even to his bicycle itself?

Is this what Albert discovered?
Does this infinite togetherness of things keep him
up at night?

Is this theory related to his socks his socks
to his wife herself to the universe?

This must be the true meaning of his Special Theory of Relativity.

Alone With Everything

Elsa decides all things are relative to this theory
as the ring on her finger is relative to her.

Is this theory just another name for a way to love
a way to dream about deserts when we walk through
rainforests?

The way she is allowed to love a tree, the small
details of light in the middle of a room
the reason of the ivy, things difficult to see.

She approaches these things with the relative
motion of love, with a heart
that longs for this theory.

This is the way she understands
what things mean to her.

The Voice of the Painter

for Sharron Antholt

for instance, a bottle of blue water in which the world floats

staying under longer for green
intermittently coming up, only for air

none of this has to be abstract

or embarrassing the way some are embarrassed to be beautiful —
unlike a schoolchild, a woman combing her hair in private

we come up against these tendrils
to set free rather than to tamp down

like some crazy unconditional love pushing up

beliefs don't matter after all
any landscape in motion spectacularly

What the Wings Look Like

Ask me if I dreamed
and I will tell you about Pablo
in the cold umber city of death.
Yes! No one knows I am a widow
who must wash her heart again
and again. I drink wine and write
letters — this grief like a bird
tearing itself from the earth's belly.
Kneeling beside his body I wonder
how the wings will look.

Transportation

If we take the train to get to Tarasçon or Rouen, then we take death to go to a star. What is certainly true in this reasoning is that while we are alive we cannot go to a star, any more than, once dead, we could catch a train.

VAN GOGH / LETTER TO THEO, 1889

I am eating the world — its corn-
fields, its black crows. I board the train in Tarasçon
for what is in your nobody's heart: a rage of work.

The first station is sorrow in its yellow house with green doors and blinds.
The second is absolute repose under a bloodred coverlet and pale
     greeny lemon sheets.

The third and last station is extreme loneliness. No one
listens. No one understands. Where is the station master in his cobalt suit?

Vermilion of the poppies.
Cypresses in this crushing prison.

One Hour of Joy

Celan and Woolf
return from their rivers
to sleep among us again.

Perhaps to find one hour of joy
and place it on each other's shoulders.

At the End of the Cold War

Sleepwalking in their bathing suits
the North Americans are back at the beach,
dreaming on thin striped towels
as if the last kiss of sun and century is theirs,

as if nothing will change

cold war, dreams of malice
shining convenient hum of more.

Native in its greed
for so long, a country
breaks the private heart.

there is not enough   there is not enough

∾

Love, love
when you wake us
when you hold our face in your hands,
we want to rise up
into the real air of your touch and laugh
at everything that is not the law of happiness.

Drenched in sun, we are
nowhere else but here

lit in ourselves
at the end of the cold war.

Stieglitz Marries Her Hands

Finally, he forgets the names
of the things he sees and marries
her hands flowering in the light.

Tonight I Am Mrs. Lorca

Blood weddings! Blood weddings!
Tonight I am Mrs. Lorca in a tight black dress with rhinestone buttons.
Beneath a thin strand of electric lights, Federico and I dance
for all the poets in the world. We throw our heads back in sweaty joy,
horses galloping on music. *Everyone is alive. Look.*
Look at the way we love.

Which Wants To

for Britt Block

The open field in the open heart
which wants to

kiss the possible
and the impossible

at once in a rush
of breath. All the hands

cradle, that the lungs
assert, a pearl of giving

and receiving all day
all night, alone in the bath

of skylight, starlight
a woman steps like a crane

into imaginary water
flowing all around her.

Balance, steady breath,
hands gentle,

wander
into me further, please

further here and here
as alive as Tosca

before her last leap
onto the apocryphal trampoline.

That lingering leap carried
safe inside, I hang glide

from an Alp in a fierce quiet moment.
Crushed silk blows

in the breeze that touches
the arm and all

it manifests.
The spirit leaves the body

when it can't stay
dishonest in its motions,

sweep its hair
across another belly

or dilate its heart.
Protect

my solitude, a summer
harvest here at the pinnacle

of heat. The bales,
fly through blue

sky like gymnasts
before the suck of gravity.

Part Five

Falling Into and Out of

1

Falling into that shivering
creature between the hushed fields,
each day takes so much of me down with it.
This is logical. This is what happens.
It is not like a glass of water or a migrating bird
though these too are miracles. Falling is imbedded,
the way an onion might be imbedded inside
the stomach of a wolf. If you ask but why would a wolf
swallow an onion, then you are getting closer to falling.
Think through the fur to the skin, through the organs
of hunger, through each sweating layer of onion
skin to the soon invisible heart. Can you tell if I'm lying?

writing, falling
falling into the words
slipping away, that is, growing older

The man beside me has written five letters.
Perhaps telling people that he is coming
the way Icarus might have. Now that I'm in the air
the whole attempt seems possible. Looking down
at the desert. The man across the aisle is playing with his
calculator. Others are playing cards. We are falling.

2

The pink teacup or is it sherbet?
A sailboat of flesh.

Houses emerge from the weave of canvas —
The difference between what is good and what is a dream?

The eucalyptus grows here.
Eucalyptus at Montalban 1917

By 1920, the blues are darker, the women sitting,
resting, holding violins.

Penciled apples in the blue bowl.

Interior, Flowers and Parrots 1924

The Rumanian Blouse 1936

The Purple Robe 1937

Woman with Philodendron 1938

Striped Blouse and Anemones 1940

Flowers become fruit become wallpaper.

How to explain to a long unseen friend simultaneous exhaustion, joy.

I kneel in front of a painting. (Hear footsteps) Look
over and see gray wool kneesocks inside leopard skin
high heels. Dare myself not to look up but do. She's
beautiful, severe. Now Birkenstocks, etc.

Read her manuscript. Mozart's playing. The faucet
dribbles. Margaret Drabble was in Italy this summer.

1947—*The Background, Red and Green* is much more,
much deeper than *Two Girls*.

3

Emergency Exit
Oxygen Mask
Life Preserver

With me it is always one or the other, falling into,
falling out of. This is logical. This is what happens.
She was never a tender room though I tried to book reservations.
Not an easy place for holidays. But my name is known.
My habits accepted.

all those years
lost writing
falling into out of
each other
Mother

watches the birds at the feeder. During lunch
she says, *those plants need new pots, more room.* Looking
for the scissors, I see she keeps my letters in the drawer
beside her bed. From up here

I am the alluvial plain, you are a beautiful
and slow glacier. No longer a blue silk parachute,
an amniotic hammock. Over the years, you reveal yourself.
We are falling together.

Is it the complexity
we love the way
one thing moves
inside another?

~~Grief~~

1

One heart, hers, in a bright leaf
calls everywhere I go
thirsty, alone
without a word for *home*,
without her but with her
flame.

2

Some days, I can only reach its farthest edge
and I have to ask myself where I am.
What answer do I have?
That the summer is cold and we are
jewels. That one eye
is blinded by sorrow.

3

Who will see me now, my lightning bolt, my opera?
Who will show me who I am?
Who will bathe me and sleep nearby to hear my first question?
Who will rub my feet and comb my thin hair?
Who will eat the bread I have made?
Who will take the furniture from the house?
Who will that be, beloved?

4

The actions of your whole life take new form
in the air near the Queen Anne's lace,
the red bed nobody sleeps in. You become a bird
flying toward what you love singing
don't cry or else
cry.

5

Help me remember
how joy begins in the middle of sorrow.

Wrapped in warm sheets to see your sister's hair,
your mother's hand with nothing in it.

What did you lose?
Where are all the lost things?

6

I am finally carried by the one I love who wears a red robe
    from her youth.
As if I am the one who prepares to leave, she carries me
toward something we can't see yet. To soothe me,
she tells me I am as light as a thousand moths floating near their flame.

7

July's nearly gone — hear the sound of wings
folded in the field — its fetal taste, crescent
flame. Where are you?
Inside the tan and silver fox?
Inside the lost daughter who is too far away?
In every embrace and sip of air?
In each naked joy that ploughs the spine?

8

We imagine how to live on earth.
In what city will death find us
and carry us over? Alone
in my chair, I listen and wait for you
to return as jazz in broad daylight.

Suffering falls away,
thin paper sheaves. Each day
becomes each day.

I lose your fragile tether as someone will
lose mine. You let go
of your body, I scatter
your white ash on the water and find a boat
that bears no footprints —

White sails on fire —
You become the water and I the boat.

Inland Beachchair

Sitting in a striped beachchair, slung low, perhaps this
is the recipe for thrills on a hot day so hot that

many whom I have desired would whisper
if you love me, you won't

touch me. I think of Van Gogh first, then William Hurt
    and Kathleen Turner
bathing in the tub of ice cubes before he questioned the downside
    of lust. Everyone's

pleasure is brief because life is short and wounding even if you're
    only slightly
intimate. Vincent, on the other hand, painted pure intimacy,
    a true wedding

of things-just-as-they-were, glazing and re-glazing for luminosity
    otherwise
known as trust. I'd like ecstasy but swore off heavy narcotics
    for a few days.

Healing, I'm in the beachchair forever, blinded by a flowering sun.

Shapes

What the eye touches first touches the infinite.
Lilac in the hand, lilac in the wallpaper.
Seeing shapes on shapes —
mother-father in first light,
breast on hand on lip on bowl.

A mother's head says a name
that becomes mine
that becomes me —
sexual like an ancient fountain in the middle of a city.
Years later, tonight

in the last light of a summer evening,
I as I
hear the loud angel
in the crow, the zucchini, the iris oh
fireflies awake the dark.

The New City

Where in such bright heat you grow
    into me where I live, who straddled
an hour, a long
    minute leaning back
between the legs you must cling to
    as you breathe another heat that is a body
in its essential hunger. A slow rocking.
    An upturning. Baffled.

    It does matter how we create
the new city which is touch, invented
    with each finger, each strand
of hair that wants this very now.
    Wing on wing, open hand
hard on your arching hip.

Look

Perhaps Rilke is everything, even a woman.
You followed her once, you saw her roses once.

They tell me only that you will smile with your whole face.
Later, this proves to be true.

Clinging to nakedness,
I wear two colors to meet you.

My ridiculous white shirt of hope gives me away,
black corduroy pants.

Intimate with the same dead, we are a society.
Inside a word: *Stonehenge.*

Our dark house,
rooms where truth hardly matters.

Water of Praise

One world filters
into the next
as when spring

returns for a day
at the end of June
or a parent becomes

someone
always leaving
childhood.

The cool clear
water of praise
rises to the surface

waking into an opening
sound
more human.

∾

To emerge from
the conflict, the door
must be kept

open and everything
should be a little deeper.
Everyone's transparent

as the infinite
falling away of light
in the first frame

prepares us for
gloomy weather
on the moor.

∾

Jean discusses getting
a flat-top
though her new leather

jacket conveys it
accoutrement for the spirit
always ready

to C'EST MOI at last.
Stick a tiger lily behind one
ear and feel

beautiful. Animal
sparks fly around the thin hold
of technology, arouse

your primitive.
Today's lesson
will be about sea

legs. Clap
and shout under
a cold

shower: bathe
in the light
of the burning star

in another
medium. I'm lonely
like this but

not for long or
for the reason
I think.

Again
the past is not
here, veering.

A Flock of Doubts Flying Beyond
the Given Boundaries

Remove the size ten shoe box
from the back of the closet and a female
ego floats out for higher
terrain. Her red scarf senses
the first release and flutters
like Garbo on a solitary stroll.

the words

experience fearlessness and raw delight

are sewn into the fabric
by whose barely perceptible hand?

     ∾

Joanne started late without regrets.
After months of days and nights in
the studio she announced, "I'm successful
with yellow." There on one flat plane, three:
unmistakable, yellow, mathematical, mysterious.

     ∾

Ten years ago someone wrote once to say:

"Your form is not yet equal to your vision."

Thin form vs thick vision
these things can't stay
separate any longer, one outside the other.

∽

When Sharron arrives at the boathouse, she's in her red
bathing suit with spaghetti straps. We swim our usual
distance, our talking heads snailing across the surface
our bodies swallowed. Suddenly, wind on the lake
and we are
fighting for home.

∽

Home is always changing form
where I am: the ocean
where I am
on my own.

Notes

"Wild Strawberries" page 3
George Costakis, born in Moscow in 1911, collected over 5,000 Russian avant-garde paintings before and after the Revolution. When he left Russia in 1977, he brought only a fraction of his collection with him which I saw at an exhibition in Stockholm in 1983.

"Why Didn't They Hear the Sea Calling?" page 11
The title is a line from John Cheever's *Falconer* (Knopf, 1977).

"Willoughby, Virginia" page 12
the bright world / the beauteous fields is from a traditional Appalachian folk song.

"Entering the Clear Space" page 17
jar of air and *door partly open* are titles from the work of the sculptor Deborah Whitman to whom I am indebted.

"The Dream" page 18
Susan Unterberg's photographs and installations have been shown at The Lawrence Miller Gallery and The New Museum in New York City.

"Wanting What is Barely Seen" page 22
Who will buoy me up is derived from one of the many insightful questions Rachel Blau du Plessis asks about the poet H.D. in "Family, Sexes, Psyche: An Essay on H.D. and the Muse of the Women Writer" from *The Pink Guitar: Writing as Feminist Practice* (Routledge, 1990).

"Friendship Among Women" page 29
we enter it and it is our home is from Mary Oppen's "Dreams" from *Poems and Transpositions* (Montemora Supplement, 1980).

"Mrs. Einstein" page 43
Elsa was Albert's second wife. It was the collaboration with his first wife Mileva Marić while they were physics students which produced "The Special Theory of Relativity"; she received no credit for her contributions to their research.

"What the Wings Look Like" page 47
I am indebted to the painter Rosa Valado for the central image in this poem.

"Transportation" page 48
In addition to the epigraph, the phrases *rage of work, yellow house with green door and blinds, absolute repose, pale greeny lemon,* and *bloodred coverlet* come from Van Gogh's letters some of which are collected in *Artists by Themselves: Van Gogh* edited by Rachel Barnes (Knopf, 1990).

"Grief" page 60
The idea that a line crossing out the word grief could become the title for the sequence is Marcie Hershman's.